DUCK

LIFE CYCLES

Words that look like **this** can be found in the glossary on page 24.

BookLife PUBLISHING

©2019
BookLife Publishing Ltd.
King's Lynn
Norfolk PE30 4LS

All rights reserved.
Printed in Malaysia.

A catalogue record for this book is available from the British Library.

ISBN: 978-1-78637-733-3

Written by:
Shalini Vallepur

Edited by:
William Anthony

Designed by:
Danielle Jones

All facts, statistics, web addresses and URLs in this book were verified as valid and accurate at time of writing. No responsibility for any changes to external websites or references can be accepted by either the author or publisher.

CONTENTS

Page 4   What Is a Life Cycle?
Page 5   What Is a Duck?
Page 6   Eggs
Page 8   Incubation
Page 10 Ducklings
Page 12 Leaving the Nest
Page 14 Ducks
Page 16 Types of Duck
Page 18 Duck Facts
Page 20 World Record Breakers
Page 22 Life Cycle of a Duck
Page 23 Get Exploring!
Page 24 Glossary and Index

WHAT IS A LIFE CYCLE?

All animals, plants and humans go through different stages of their life as they grow and change. This is called a life cycle.

Human life cycle

Baby → Child → Adult

WHAT IS A DUCK?

A duck is a type of bird. Ducks have beaks, **waterproof** feathers and webbed feet that help them to swim.

Most adult ducks can fly.

EGGS

Female ducks lay their eggs in a nest. They build the nest out of sticks, grass and leaves.

Some ducks use their own feathers in the nest.

Eggs are laid in the warmer months of the year.
Some types of duck lay more eggs than other ducks.

A group of eggs is called a clutch.

INCUBATION

The female duck keeps her eggs warm by sitting on them. This is called incubation.

To find food, mother ducks will leave their eggs.

A baby duck is called a duckling. The duckling grows inside the egg for around a month.

Yolk

Duckling

Ducklings feed on the <u>yolk</u> inside the egg.

DUCKLINGS

A duckling has a sharp egg tooth. They use it to break out of the egg. The tooth falls off after the duckling has hatched.

Egg tooth

When ducklings hatch, they are wet. They stay in the nest for about ten hours to dry off and rest.

Ducklings are covered with soft, fluffy down.

LEAVING THE NEST

After a while, the ducklings are ready to leave the nest for the first time. Their mother takes them to the nearest body of water.

Young ducklings can't fly, so they have to walk.

Jump in!

Once they make it to water, the ducklings learn what to eat and have their first swim. Ducks are **omnivores**. They eat seeds, plants and insects.

DUCKS

Ducklings grow adult feathers when they are around two months old. That is when most types of duck will be able to fly.

Adult duck feathers are waterproof.

After a year, the fully grown ducks are ready to find a **mate**. Females will build nests, ready for eggs.

Male and female ducks form a bond.

TYPES OF DUCK

There are over 100 different **species** of duck. Ducks can be found all over the world, except in Antarctica. They come in lots of different colours.

The male ruddy duck has a bright blue beak.

The male mandarin duck has many beautiful colours.

Most male ducks have colourful feathers to attract female ducks. A male duck is called a drake and a female duck is called a duck or a hen.

17

DUCK FACTS

Have you ever wondered why ducklings follow their mother everywhere? Ducklings become **attached** to the first thing they see when they hatch – their mother!

They follow her wherever she goes.

Some ducks eat by dabbling. The duck dips its head underwater to reach plants but keeps its bottom in the air.

WORLD RECORD BREAKERS

World's Oldest Duck

The oldest known duck was a mallard called Desi. She was 20 years old. Mallard ducks usually live to be around five to ten years old.

Fast Fliers

Ducks are very good at flying. The red-breasted merganser can fly at around 130 kilometres per hour!

LIFE CYCLE OF A DUCK

1 Female ducks lay their eggs in a nest.

2 The female duck incubates the eggs for about 30 days until they hatch.

LIFE CYCLES

3 The ducklings walk to the water. They grow adult feathers.

4 After a year they are ready to find a mate.

Get Exploring!

Have you ever seen a duck where you live? There might be some at a pond, or you could visit a petting zoo to learn more about ducks. Always take care around the water!

GLOSSARY

attached　　not wanting to be away from something or someone

bond　　form a close relationship

down　　small, fluffy and fine feathers

mate　　a partner (of the same species) that an animal chooses to produce young with

omnivores　　animals that eat both plants and animals

species　　a group of very similar animals or plants that can produce young together

waterproof　　something that water cannot pass through

yolk　　the yellow part of an egg

INDEX

beaks 5, 16
dabbling 19
down 11
ducklings 9–14, 18, 22
eggs 6–10, 15, 22
feathers 5–6, 14, 17, 22
fly 5, 12, 14, 21
incubation 8, 22
mallards 20
mates 15, 22
nests 6, 11–12, 15, 22
swimming 5, 13, 19
water 12–13, 19, 22–23

PHOTO CREDITS

All images are courtesy of Shutterstock.com, unless otherwise specified. With thanks to Getty Images, Thinkstock Photo and iStockphoto. Front cover – Oleksandr Lytvynenko Erica Truex. 1 – Oleksandr Lytvynenko Erica Truex. 2 – Ondrej Chvatal. 3 – koosen, Sascha Burkard, Robert Eastman1. 4 – Intellistudies, michaeljung, India Picture, Bahruz Rzayev. 5 – rck_953. 6 – Maksimilian. 7 – Vishnevskiy Vasily. 8 – aleksander hunta. 9 – BlueRingMedia. 10 – Tim Belyk. 11 – Alexander Bente. 12 – CreativeMedia.org.uk. 13 – Mircea Costina. 14 – Rotter. 15 – CoolR. 16 – Alina Kurbiel. 17 – BOONCHUAY PROMJIAM. 18 – evastudio. 19 – Daniel-Alvarez. 20 – Maquiladora, robuart, Valerii_M. 21 – Maquiladora. 22 –norawish dittanet, Anneka, Katie Richardson, Leka Sergeeva. 23 – Keith Publicover.